KU-112-694

I am God's Masterpiece

Written & Illustrated
by Desola Adeniyi

Copyright © 2023
Desola Adeniyi
All rights reserved. No part of this book may be reproduced or distributed in any form without any prior written consent from the publisher.

"I am God's masterpiece. I am fearfully and wonderfully made."
(Psalm 139:14)

"I am crowned with glory and honour."
(Psalm 8:5)

"I am brave and will fear no evil."
(Psalm 23:4)

"I am loved and the apple of God's eye."
(Zechariah 2:8)

"I deserve love, peace and joy."
(John 14:27)

"I can do all things through Christ who strengthens me." (Philippians 4:13)

"I am safe and protected by God."
(2 Thessalonians 3:3)

"I have been blessed with a beautiful gift called life."
(Psalm 129:14)

"I have a bright future ahead of me."
(Romans 8:28)

"I am capable of making a positive difference
in the world."
(Matthew 28:18-20)

"I am not afraid because
I put my trust in God."
(Psalm 56:3)

"I am the head and not the tail. I am destined for great things." (Deuteronomy 28:13)

Printed in Great Britain
by Amazon

39537819R00018